Original title:
Banana Bounty

Copyright © 2025 Creative Arts Management OÜ
All rights reserved.

Author: Rosalie Bradford
ISBN HARDBACK: 978-1-80586-370-0
ISBN PAPERBACK: 978-1-80586-842-2

Orchard of Joy

In the orchard where laughter sways,
Fruit hangs low on sunny days.
Monkeys swing, they steal a bite,
Chasing squirrels in sheer delight.

With a grin, I grab a snack,
The juicy goodness, no lack.
Sticky fingers, sweet surprise,
In this place, my spirit flies.

Golden Harvest Dance

Underneath the big, blue sky,
We gather round as spirits fly.
Gather 'round for a juicy treat,
Dance along to nature's beat.

Laughter echoes, a playful race,
Fruit juice dribbles down my face.
With every twist and silly prance,
Joy springs forth in this harvest dance.

Underneath the Canopy

Underneath the leafy shade,
Silly shadows waltz and play.
A hidden stash, so sweet and bright,
Beneath the leaves, what a sight!

Juggling fruits, a comical show,
Laughter bursts, it's quite the glow.
Nature's gifts, a playful spree,
Join the fun, come climb with me.

The Fruitful Feast

Gather 'round, it's feast time here,
With fruity treats and lots of cheer.
Spoons and forks may not apply,
Let's dig in, oh me, oh my!

Chomp and munch, I take a bite,
Everything tastes just so right.
Laughter shared, it can't be beat,
A joyful feast that can't be beat.

The Delightful Sway

In the trees, they dance and swing,
Yellow blurs like socks in spring.
With a chuckle, they twist and bend,
A fruity joke that doesn't end.

While monkeys laugh and share a tease,
Who knew a snack could bring such ease?
Peel and bite, the flavor's bold,
Sit back, relax, let laughter unfold.

Treasure in the Green

Under leaves, a hidden prize,
A quirky fruit beneath the skies.
Not gold, but yellow, smooth, and sweet,
A treasure map that leads to treat!

With every munch, a giggle flows,
A fruity riddle no one knows.
In this jungle, we will play,
A fruity jest on a sunny day.

Currents of Flavor

Waves of taste, a playful ride,
A slippery treat, full of pride.
In a bowl, they leap and dive,
Creating smiles, they come alive!

With every bite, a joke does land,
A comedy act from nature's hand.
Giggles burst while taste buds sing,
In this fruity, fun-filled fling.

Garden of Whimsy

In a patch where giggles grow,
A yellow charm puts on a show.
With every pluck, a laugh appears,
Echoing through the sunny years.

They wobble and wobble, oh so round,
Creating chaos, joy abound.
In this garden, fun's the aim,
Each vibrant fruit plays its game.

The Fabled Yellow Treasure

In jungles deep, a treasure hides,
With wrinkled skin, it laughs and chides.
A fruit so bright, it steals the show,
A silly sight, when monkeys throw.

This yellow charm invites a bite,
Giggles burst like morning light.
It spins a tale of fruity fun,
In every peel, a pun begun.

Dancing in the Summer Breeze

With laughter loud, the fruit does sway,
As breezes chase the heat away.
A twisty dance, a playful fling,
The summer calls, and joy takes wing.

A bunch of smiles in golden hue,
They roll and tumble like a crew.
In every bite, a giggle found,
Life's sweetest joy, so round and sound.

Golden Glades of Joy

In sunny fields, where laughter grows,
A treasure glows, a sweet repose.
With every munch, a chuckle springs,
Oh what delight this silly brings!

The yellow orbs in gleeful play,
Invite the critters out to sway.
In grassy nests, the puns will fly,
As frolicsome friends all munch and sigh.

Echoes of Fruity Abundance

In markets bright, they start the chatter,
With silly jingles, causing clatter.
A fruit parade, a vibrant feast,
From tiny nibble to mighty beast!

Each slice and bite, a joyful cheer,
Echoes of laughter, far and near.
A banquet filled with giggling zest,
The fruity fun, forever blessed.

Echoes of Abundance

In a land where fruit is king,
All the monkeys dance and sing.
Peeling laughter in the air,
While monkeys swing without a care.

Golden treasures on each tree,
Hanging like a comedy spree.
Forks and spoons, they steal away,
To feast and joke, it's their buffet.

With every slip and joyful fall,
Their chatter rings, a merry call.
Chasing dreams that taste so sweet,
They prance and play with happy feet.

So let us giggle, share a bite,
In this fruity, funny sight.
As the sun sets, laughter flows,
A harvest full of silly woes.

The Ripe Journey

On a quest for golden cheer,
Traveling far, from far and near.
Each twist and turn, a wild ride,
With slip-ups that could make you hide.

In the jungle, oh what fun,
Chasing shadows, on the run.
A furry friend, a cheeky prank,
Brought us joy and laughter's bank.

With every step, we share our snack,
No one minds if we lose track.
Tales of mishaps fill the night,
As we munch under starlight.

So when life tosses you a chance,
Grab a fruit, and do a dance.
In silly moments, joy is found,
With every giggle, we astound.

Sunlit Splendor Beneath the Canopy

In the jungle, a slip and a slide,
A yellow fruit takes you for a ride.
Monkeys giggle, oh what a sight,
Chasing shadows, feeling just right.

Under leaves, the laughter resounds,
Fruit-shaped treasures are always found.
With every bite, a joke, a cheer,
Sweetness wrapped in giggles so dear.

A Symphony of Yellow Delight

A fruit orchestra plays in the sun,
Silly percussion, oh what fun!
Each peel flings jokes into the air,
Laughter and giggles everywhere.

A comedy show, spontaneous and bright,
With every fruit, a punchline in sight.
Twirling in circles, the fun won't cease,
In the fruity realm, there's joy and peace.

Tropics of Gold

In golden groves, where giggles grow,
Each ripe treat puts on quite a show.
Slip on a peel, watch your friends fall,
Laughter erupts, it's a party, y'all!

Chasing shadows as the swings fly high,
With fruity friends, we reach for the sky.
Under the sun, mischief will reign,
Every slip and slide feels like champagne!

Harvested Dreams

In orchards bright, where the fun unfolds,
Laughter blooms like the sun that holds.
Peeling layers, oh what surprise,
Under the sky, with joyful cries.

Gather your pals, it's time to feast,
A fruity picnic, laughter unleashed.
With every nibble, a giggle ignites,
In this harvest, pure joy ignites.

Sorrows of a Wilted Leaf

A leaf once vibrant, now all brown,
Gossip spreads as it flops down.
"Why so wilted?" the stalk does tease,
"Got too much sun and not much breeze."

The ants parade with tiny frowns,
While mushrooms giggle, pushing crowns.
"Looks like you've had quite the affair,
With the sun too hot, oh, do beware!"

Tiny raindrops mock from above,
"Dancing all day, yet no true love!"
A wilted sigh escapes its stem,
Oh, the tales that leaf will condemn!

Yet in its heart, a secret glows,
Dreams of dancing in summer's throes.
With humor wrapped in yellow cheer,
It chuckles softly, "I'll persevere!"

Feast in the Sunlit Grove

In the grove where giggles burst,
Fruit hangs low, oh what a thirst!
Squirrels dart with acorn glee,
While shadows whisper, "Come, just see!"

The sunbeams slide on crispy grass,
As critters scheme to have a blast.
A feast awaits, all flavors bright,
One berry's sweet, the other's slight!"

Laughter rings through twisted vines,
Frogs croak jingles, weaving signs.
With every nibble, every bite,
Tummy grumbles echo delight!

Watch as laughter rolls like waves,
In the sunlit, shade-filled enclaves.
Who knew a picnic could ignite,
Such joy in every silly bite?

Tropical Mirth and Melodies

In tropic lands, where colors play,
The fruits hum tunes throughout the day.
A mango twirls, a lime does sing,
In harmony, they dance in spring.

Coconuts giggle high on trees,
While parrots tease with silly wheeze.
A pineapple struts with regal flair,
Sporting a crown without a care!

Beneath the sun's warm, cheerful beam,
The fruits unite in sweetest dream.
Together they sway with breezy grace,
In this paradise, smiles embrace.

Guitar strums from a lizard band,
As critters gather to clap their hands.
In this jungle of joy, so wild and free,
The fruit party rolls eternally!

Curves of Joy

In orchards sweet, where laughter grows,
Curved delights hang in sunny rows.
Wiggly worms join the festive swirl,
As the fruits nudge, and giggles twirl.

Chubby cheeks, with sticky hands,
Create a ruckus in fruit-filled lands.
A silly bug waltzes in place,
With wobbly moves, it finds its space.

Fuzzy peaches whisper secrets bright,
While nectarines engage in light.
Curves of happiness sway with ease,
In this treasure trove of fruity tease.

Ripe with flavor, joy will abide,
In every laugh, there's sweetness inside.
So take a bite of nature's grin,
And let the jolly fest begin!

Ripened Dreams

In the kitchen, fruits collide,
A yellow grin I cannot hide.
Peels around, a slippery floor,
I slip and slide, and then I roar!

Chasing shadows, what a scene,
A cheerful dance by Mr. Green.
Laughter spills from every space,
As I twirl with fruity grace.

Monkey business, oh so sweet,
I must admit, I can't be beat.
With every bite, a chuckle blooms,
In this world, joy surely looms.

So here's to snacks, a silly treat,
In dreams, I find my fruity feat.
A world of giggles, bright and bold,
Where ripened laughs are purest gold.

Sweetness in Every Bite

In a bowl of yellow cheer,
I've found my laughter, oh so near.
With every crunch, a burst of glee,
I munch my way to jubilee.

A fruit so sweet, it makes me sing,
In every slice, a joyful ring.
From smoothies green to pies so bright,
This golden snack brings pure delight.

As I peel the layers of my fate,
I trip on joy that feels so great.
With friends around, we share a grin,
In this sweet world, we all just win.

Life's a feast, so come take a bite,
Shimmering dreams in morning light.
With every taste, the fun ignites,
Oh, sweetness found in playful bites!

Echoes of the Tropics

Under palm trees, laughter flows,
As playful breezes gently blow.
Tropical sun, a golden hue,
With fruity giggles, we'll break through.

A fruity feast, so rich and bold,
Echoes of joy, a tale retold.
In sun-kissed lands where dreams take flight,
The tropics sing of pure delight.

With friends in tow, we take a bite,
Exploring flavors, oh what a sight!
Every chuckle, a vibrant swirl,
In this garden, let laughter unfurl.

So here beneath the azure sky,
We dance and twirl, oh me, oh my!
With every piece, a joke takes flight,
Echoes of fun, shining so bright.

The Vibrant Harvest

In fields of gold, we leap with glee,
Harvest time, come dance with me!
Nature's laughter fills the air,
A vibrant feast beyond compare.

With giggles ripe, we fill our carts,
Silly smiles, and joyful hearts.
Peeling layers of the day,
Joyful munching leads the way!

From trees above, the fruits cascade,
A frisky game, let's not evade.
With every crunch, a playful shout,
In this harvest, we throw doubt out.

So gather round, young and old,
With spirits bright, and stories told.
In every bite, laughter throngs,
A vibrant harvest where joy belongs.

Tropical Gold Rush

In a jungle dense and sweet,
The harvest joyously greets,
With monkeys dancing in delight,
Chasing fruit from morn till night.

The sun shines bright, the skies so blue,
With every peel, there's laughter too,
In this land where smiles abound,
Gold-colored gems can always be found.

The Orchard's Sweet Secret

Whispers float on a gentle breeze,
About hidden fruits among the trees,
A secret that's shared with a wink,
In this crazy orchard, come take a drink.

With every bite, a giggle springs,
As juicy laughter in the air sings,
Who knew such sweetness could exist,
When life gives you fruit, you can't resist!

Fruitful Delights Await

Gather 'round, it's time to feast,
On fruity fun, our joy increased,
With playful peels and tasty bites,
Let's celebrate under the lights!

In this garden of fruity dreams,
We'll laugh and play, or so it seems,
Each crunch a burst, a silly cheer,
It's pure delight that brings us near.

A Peel of Paradise

In a land where the fruit trees sway,
Jolly creatures come out to play,
With slippery peels that slip and slide,
Under the sun, our joy won't hide.

A comical dance on the golden ground,
We slip and tumble, laughter resounds,
In this paradise of fruity fun,
We cherish each moment, every pun!

Whispers of the Rainforest

In the jungle, monkeys play,
Swinging 'round, they shout hooray!
With a fruit in hand, they tease,
Tossing peels with crazy ease.

Laughter echoes through the trees,
As they dance upon the breeze.
Colors bright, a fruit parade,
In this leafy, wild charade.

Slips and trips, oh what a sight!
Giggling critters, pure delight.
Creatures join in this sweet spree,
Chasing rainbows, wild and free.

The rainforest's heart does sing,
Bringing forth joy like a spring.
In the chaos, we can see,
Nature's wackiest jubilee.

Peeling Back Joy

With a grin, I peel the skin,
Joy inside, where to begin?
Splitting laughter, oh so bright,
Yellow smiles in morning light.

Silly faces, a fruity fight,
Slip 'n slide, oh what a sight!
Chasing giggles, dodging mess,
Each bite brings a new success.

Squeeze the juice, let's make a toast,
To the fun we love the most!
Wacky flavors, smiles abound,
With each bite, we're glory-bound.

So pass the fruit, let's all indulge,
In this joy, we shall not bulge!
With laughter flowing, spirits high,
Peeling joy, we reach the sky!

Swaying in the Breeze

Leaves are rustling, birds take flight,
A fruity party, pure delight!
Tossed in laughter, swinging wide,
Nature's humor, no need to hide.

Down they tumble, with a grin,
Swaying gently, let's begin!
A fruity competition starts,
We dance around with open hearts.

Catch the peel—a slippery game,
A flying fruit? Oh what a claim!
Giggles bursting, wild and free,
Laughter swaying like a spree.

In the breeze, the fun takes flight,
Silly moments, pure delight.
Join the dance, just grab a friend,
Swaying 'til the very end!

Sunlit Treasures

In the sunlight, treasures gleam,
Yellow wonders, spark a dream.
Critters scamper, join the fun,
Chasing shadows, on the run.

Twisted vines, a playful race,
Bumping here, they find their place.
In the glow, a silly chase,
With each peel—a joyful face.

Sudden slips and bursts of cheer,
Nature's antics, drawing near.
A harvest rich, we laugh and dance,
In this merry, sunny trance.

So here we are with smiles so wide,
In the warmth, we take our stride.
Sunlit moments, full of glee,
Treasure found in wild decree.

Chasing Sunbeams

In a grove where shadows dance,
A monkey pranced, a merry glance.
He spotted treats, oh what a sight,
Golden delights, just pure delight.

He climbed up high, with joyful grin,
Swinging and swooping, let the fun begin.
Tripped on a leaf, fell with a thud,
Rushed to grab that sticky bud.

Back up he goes, a mischievous chase,
Friends join the fray, it's a wild race.
Laughter erupts, as they all compete,
For the sweetest prize, it can't be beat.

Underneath the sun's warm gleam,
They swing and sway, living the dream.
No frowns allowed, just giggles galore,
Chasing cheer, they always want more.

Nature's Sunlit Curvature

In a patch of golden rays,
Tiny critters dance and play.
A spider spins a web so bright,
Catching glimmers, a dazzling sight.

A curious cat with a spirited leap,
Wakes the sleepy bugs from their sleep.
Chasing shadows, oh what a mess,
What joy it brings, no time to rest!

Bright jackets flaunt, each color bold,
Nature's secrets waiting to unfold.
Grasshopper hops, a clever jest,
Wearing a hat, he's simply the best!

Laughter echoes through the trees,
As the wind hums a playful tease.
Frolicsome days, under sun's embrace,
Nature's bounty brings a smiling face.

Legends of the Lush

A tale of fruit, ripe and sweet,
With every bite, a fruity feat.
Villagers gather, a festival there,
To crown the juiciest, they share.

Old Farmer Joe, with a clever wink,
Said, "My crop makes others blink!"
His secret? A sprinkle of pure fun,
And happy thoughts under the sun.

Children giggle at silly tricks,
Blaming their pals for the sticky licks.
From pies to shakes, they create with glee,
Legends arise, as grand as can be.

With joyous hearts and laughter loud,
They celebrate, all feeling proud.
A harmony born from nature's zest,
Creating moments that never rest.

Clusters of Sunshine

In the fields where delights grow,
Bubbles of laughter, a sunny show.
Frogs on lily pads, wearing crowns,
Sing silly songs as the world spins 'round.

Clusters hang bright, a fragrant dream,
Splashes of joy with every beam.
Squirrels leap, their acrobatics tease,
Chasing each other, dancing with ease.

Picnics planned with treats galore,
Sticky fingers wanting more.
Smiles so wide, a contagious spread,
As food and laughter fill each head.

The sun dips low, a golden ball,
Chasing shadows, they'll never fall.
Under a sky of painted hue,
Clusters of sunshine, forever true.

The Golden Horizon

In a fruit bowl, there's a prize,
A yellow gem that catches eyes.
When you peel back its bright attire,
It's the treasure we all desire.

Slip on peels, they take a dive,
Everyone laughs, they feel alive.
A fruit so silly, it can't be still,
Dancing and bouncing, what a thrill!

On sunny days, they hang around,
Swinging softly, never a frown.
Chasing each other, what a sight,
A fruity party, pure delight!

So let's toast with a yellow cheer,
To the fruit that brings us near.
With laughter echoing through the air,
Golden dreams, without a care!

Nature's Sweet Ode

In the orchard, sweetness grows,
Curvy shapes in rows and rows.
With every bite, a giggle springs,
Nature's gift with funny flings.

Splash the juice, it drips and drizzles,
Messy faces cause the giggles.
Bananas laughing in my hand,
Wobbling like a dancing band!

They wear a coat of sunny cheer,
A fruity smile, oh so dear.
When left too long, they turn to mush,
Yet still they bring a joyful hush!

So let us sing, with voices bright,
To the fruit that brings us light.
With every munch, a chuckle flows,
In nature's joy, the laughter grows!

Petals of Joy

In verdant realms where laughter thrives,
A quirky fruit with jolly jives.
Wrapped in sunshine, sweet and bold,
Its quirky charm never gets old.

Peels that slip with playful grace,
Spinning in a goofy race.
One small trip, and down they go,
Giggles echo as they show!

Each bite bursts with a zingy thrill,
Round and yellow, they fit the bill.
A snack tucked in, a pocket bright,
Bringing joy, oh what a sight!

So gather round, let's all partake,
In this merry fruit-filled wake.
With laughter shared, our spirits soar,
In the fruity fun, who could ask for more?

Curves of Nectar

In gardens where the sunshine beams,
Curvy wonders fulfill our dreams.
With every peel, a joyful grin,
This playful fruit, let the fun begin!

Fumbling feasts with sticky hands,
Nature's laughter fills our lands.
Rolling, tumbling, down the street,
A fruity treasure, oh so sweet!

Overripe and slightly brown,
They wear a silly, squishy crown.
Not just a snack, but a party cue,
In every bite, a laugh rings true!

So let's celebrate our fruity friends,
Where every giggle simply blends.
In every curve, a joke to find,
A sweet delight that's one of a kind!

Laughter Among the Leaves

Under the tree, a giggle grows,
Yellow hats dance, full of woes.
Bunches swing in the gentle breeze,
Tickling toes and causing unease.

Silly monkeys hold a feast,
Swinging high, they munch at least.
With every chomp, a chuckle flies,
Fruitful antics under bright blue skies.

The squirrels join, debate the taste,
Waging war in this fruity haste.
Peeled delights, a slippery race,
Rolling down with silly grace.

In shade of gold, all bounce around,
With merry hearts, no frowns are found.
Nature's jesters, fun on display,
Laughter blooms in a bright array.

The Sunny Haven

In the garden, sunshine beams,
Golden peels and funny dreams.
Colors clash, a vivid sight,
Laughing fruits in pure delight.

Chortles echo in bright hues,
Shadows dance, the day ensues.
Sticky fingers, joyful cheer,
As laughter ripens year by year.

Buzzing bees play their sweet tune,
Joking with the sun and moon.
Here and there, a playful plop,
Fruit falls down with a funny flop.

Friends unite in this bright space,
Every smile, a warm embrace.
Jests mix with the scents of fun,
A bright haven, joy to run.

Fruitful Visions

In a land of yellow mirth,
Silly creatures, full of girth.
Jumping high with peels to throw,
Chasing dreams, they put on a show.

Curly tails and playful eyes,
Rolling laughter fills the skies.
Every bite brings a new grin,
Happiness in every spin.

The parade marches, oh so grand,
With fruity crowns and laughter planned.
Bumbling bugs join the spree,
Swirling dizzily, oh so free.

In this realm of yellow cheer,
Life's a dance, and joy is near.
Imagining tales, so light and bright,
Where laughter reigns and hearts take flight.

The Melody of Sunshine

A symphony of fruity cheer,
Melodies that tickle the ear.
Swinging branches hum a tune,
With each strum, the hearts commune.

Tiny critters join the beat,
Dancing fast on happy feet.
The fruit sings as it swings low,
In this show, the laughs will flow.

Buzz and laughter fill the air,
Playful vibes are everywhere.
Jingling laughter fills the grove,
In this rhythm, joy will rove.

Sunrays painting golden smiles,
Happiness stretching for miles.
Join the chorus, don't delay,
In the sunny groove, let's play!

Sun-dappled Delicacies

In the shade where laughter grows,
A fruit hangs low with a silly pose.
Slip and slide, the yellow dreams,
As monkeys giggle in sunlight beams.

Peel away the giggling skin,
Squishy delights, let the fun begin.
With every bite, a chuckle bursts,
Sweetness blooms, and joy it thrusts.

Chasing shadows, we dance and twirl,
Fruity treats make our heads whirl.
In the orchard, we play all day,
A comical feast in a sunny spray.

Lush Fruit, Laughter, and Life

Swinging high among the leaves,
A playful bunch that never grieves.
With each peel, a giggly sound,
In this jungle, joy abounds.

Mischief hides in every bite,
A slippery prize, oh what a sight!
Dancing vines, we laugh so loud,
Jumpy antics, we're fruit proud.

Tropical tales beneath the sun,
In the orchard, it's all just fun.
Life is sweet with every taste,
We savor joy and never waste.

The Joyous Harvest Dance

Gather round for the harvest cheer,
A fruit fiesta, come lend an ear!
Laughter bubbles, ripe and bright,
As we celebrate with sheer delight.

The fruity jig, a slippery show,
Twists and turns, with a dash and a glow.
In golden sun, we shimmy and sway,
With every leg, we peel away!

Bunches of giggles, tangle your hair,
Let's bounce around without a care.
A harvest dance with friends so dear,
The joy and laughter bring us near.

Golden Whispers After Rain

Pitter-patter, the sky drizzles,
Golden treats with sparkly twizzles.
Sunshine glimmers on the slick ground,
A fruity grin all around.

Raindrops fade, the world is bright,
With every glisten, pure delight.
Nature chuckles, a cheeky fling,
Whispers of joy in the spring.

Slip and slide on the muddy path,
Just look at us, we're full of laughs!
In the lush garden, we simply play,
Chasing fun, come what may.

From the Earth's Embrace

A yellow curve upon the vine,
Bright laughter ripens, oh so fine.
The monkey grins, it's time to feast,
With every bite, joy is released.

Swinging high from tree to tree,
A jungle jig, just you and me.
With sticky fingers, we delight,
In nature's candy, pure and bright.

The sun now sets, the day is done,
Chasing dreams, we made our fun.
In the twilight, giggles blend,
To the lull of fruits that never end.

Harvesting Sunshine

Golden gifts on swinging shade,
In every twist, a joke is laid.
With a peel that slips and slides,
The laughter grows as each one bides.

A comedy of slips and trips,
As we gather our fruity quips.
Sunny smiles upon our faces,
We dance around in nature's graces.

The jungle sings, it's quite a show,
Each tangy bite, a wave of glow.
Like little secrets from the sun,
In these moments, we are one.

Dreams in Every Bite

In sleep's embrace, we dream of cheer,
Of silly tastes that bring us near.
A creamy galaxy awaits, oh please,
As we munch away with joy and ease.

The pudding dance, the frosty treat,
All wrapped up in yellow heat.
With every nibble, giggles grow,
In a world where fruits steal the show.

Laughter echoes, fills the air,
As fruity wishes whisk us there.
In every bite, the joy ignites,
A fruity dream that never bites.

The Lure of the Tropics

An island breeze, the tale unfolds,
Of fruity treasures that the sun holds.
With each burst of sunshine sweet,
We march along with silly feet.

The lure of yellow brings a cheer,
With warming rays, it draws us near.
We play along like kids at play,
As nectar dreams brighten the day.

In every nook, a laughter rings,
As we crown our heads with fruity things.
The tropics hum a merry tune,
As we feast beneath the glowing moon.

Bounty of the Tropics

In the land where sunbeams dance,
Yellow fruits sit in a trance.
Monkeys chatter, but who would care,
When snacks are ripe and everywhere.

Peeling back the golden skin,
A slippery giggle is sure to win.
With every bite, it's joy that's shared,
This fruit's the prize that's never scared.

Sipping smoothies, laughing loud,
Underneath that leafy shroud.
In a fruit bowl, it claims its throne,
The tropics' laugh, its sweetest tone.

So let us cheer for tropic cheer,
With vibrant fruit and friends so dear.
In every munch and every crunch,
Who knew delight was in one bunch!

The Abundant Harvest

When harvest time comes rolling in,
Yellow smiles are sure to win.
From trees above, they tumble down,
The fruit parade in nature's gown.

With every slip and every fall,
We're echoing joy, hear the call!
Try to stack them in a pile,
Good luck, my friend, it's quite the trial!

In pancakes stacked, or pudding shared,
The sweetness lingers, none compared.
Every dish, a happy fate,
With laughter served upon the plate.

So raise a toast to all that's bright,
This fruity feast is sheer delight.
Let's dance around, give all a cheer,
For golden joy that's always near!

Sweetness in Every Curve

In curves of gold, such playful tease,
This fruit brings laughter with such ease.
Sitting high in cheerful trees,
It beckons all, 'Come share with me!'

With goofy peels and squishy bites,
It bounces back, such silly sights.
Fruit salads flash with vibrant flair,
A giggle snack beyond compare.

When lunchtime strikes, we make a dive,
In smoothie joy, we come alive.
Chasing sweetness, no need to rush,
This fruit brings forth a happy crush.

So let's unite in fruity glee,
For curves and laughs are meant to be.
In every munch, we find our way,
To laughter's land, we dance and sway!

Nature's Curvaceous Gift

On sunny days so warm and bright,
Nature gifts us pure delight.
With every peel, the mischief starts,
The laughter flows, filling our hearts.

Silly slips and friendly grins,
The joy of munching, where it begins.
In smoothies mixed and cakes so sweet,
We find the fun, oh, what a treat!

At picnics laid on grassy green,
A yellow friend is often seen.
It rolls and rocks, a merry show,
In nature's game, it steals the glow.

So here's to curves and fruity fun,
Let's play and laugh under the sun.
With yellow joy, we sing and lift,
For nature smiles, this curvy gift!

The Yellow Oasis

In a grove of bright delight,
Yellow skins are quite the sight.
They swing and sway with such great glee,
Promise of a fruity spree.

Monkeys jest and dance around,
Chasing treats that tumble down.
With every peel, they squeal and cheer,
In this jungle, joy's the sphere.

In smoothies, pies, they take their place,
But oh, the green ones—what a waste!
They crave the sunny skins so fair,
Leaving not a speck to share.

Such laughter echoes through the land,
With every slip, they take a stand.
This golden fruit, such merry jest,
In the sunlit woods, they are the best!

Sun-Kissed Splendor

Among the trees, they laugh and play,
In sun-kissed hues, they greet the day.
Bright sunshine melts their worries away,
Fun-filled times, come join the fray!

Slip on a peel, it's quite a show,
Gravity's pull, oh don't be slow!
They giggle and roll, what a scene,
Life is grand when you're a queen!

The smoothies blend, a sweet delight,
Crisp cereal topped, oh what a sight!
Stir up some mischief with a twist,
In fruity chaos, you can't resist!

So gather round, let's have some fun,
With laughter echoing, everyone!
In this patch of joy and cheer,
We'll share the golden love right here!

Fruits of Paradise

In a land where sunlight glows,
Bright fruit laughter always flows.
Peeling back the silly skin,
Those happy bites invite a grin.

See the critters laugh and run,
In fruity games, they have their fun.
Tumbling down, they start to prance,
In purple hats, they dance and dance.

Mixing drinks that sparkle bright,
Sipping sweetness, pure delight.
Bright yellow beacons in a bowl,
They lift your heart and fill your soul!

Underneath the towering leaves,
Joyful chattering never leaves.
With every bite, a chuckle swells,
In this paradise, all is well!

Lush Laughter

In the garden of laughter loud,
Fruitful jesters drawing a crowd.
Spilling snacks and playful cheer,
Who knew yellow could bring such queer?

Playful monkeys leap with glee,
Swiping treats from you and me.
Each juicy bite a joyful shout,
They dance around, there's no doubt!

Glistening in the bright sunshine,
Whimsical tales, all intertwined.
Slipping, sliding, who will fall?
With every giggle, we stand tall!

So gather friends for fun today,
In this harvest, joy's on display.
With splendid fruit, we'll put on a show,
In this lush laughter, let's all glow!

Sunlit Surprises

In the garden bright and spry,
A yellow snack waves hello, oh my!
It giggles in the warm sun light,
Is it fruit or just pure delight?

A monkey swings by with a grin,
"Is that a snack? Let's dive right in!"
With every bite, the laughter grows,
As sweet juice drips from tiny toes.

Round and bouncy, a funny site,
Rolling by on a sunny night.
Each peel is a slip, a giggles snare,
A playful chase, what a wild dare!

Twirls and dances, the fruit's parade,
With friends and joy, the worries fade.
In this land of yellow cheer,
We'll snack, we'll laugh, in sunny sphere!

Fruitful Echoes

In the orchard where whispers sing,
Golden globes on trees do cling.
A yell of joy, a splash of cheer,
What mischief hides the fruits so near?

With pelts so slippery, ripe and plump,
Falling down with a humorous thump.
They bounce and roll, a swirling spree,
Creating giggles like a symphony.

Laughter rings out, in joyous sounds,
As antics abound, fun knows no bounds.
These fruity fellows are full of jest,
A wild sense of humor, the very best!

Echoing laughter through sunny skies,
Underneath the watchful eyes.
Silly slices, unique delight,
A fruity feast, oh what a sight!

Joyful Curves

Curvaceous curves in the afternoon,
Round and bouncy, like a tune.
Wiggling and jiggling in the sun,
Who knew fruit could be so much fun?

Swinging by, a frolicsome bunch,
Hanging high, ready for lunch!
Peels like laughter, bright and bold,
A yellow smile worth its weight in gold.

Chasing around, it's quite the race,
These joyful curves put a smile on my face.
Unpredictable like a prankster's play,
Addictive giggles make the day!

Let's savor this fun in all its glee,
A banquet of smiles, come dance with me.
In this fruity frolic, we find our bliss,
Hold on tight, don't you dare miss!

Beneath the Emerald Leaves

Hidden treasures lie below,
Under leaves where sweet fruits grow.
A tickle of joy, a pinch of fun,
Surprises linger in the sun.

Creeping critters in green disguise,
Guarding laughter with silly cries.
What fun awaits under this lush screen,
With fruity pranks, so unforeseen!

Squeezing tight in a fruity hug,
Rolling jelly legs, they give a shrug.
A splash of juice runs wild and free,
Beneath emerald leaves, here's a jubilee!

So gather round, and take a bite,
In this world so carefree and bright.
Come join the laughter, take a stand,
Under the green, it's all so grand!

Feast of the Tropics

In the shade of lush green trees,
Fruit flies dance with mighty glee.
Jungle drums beat loud and clear,
Whoops and laughter fill the sphere.

Chefs in hats, so tall and bright,
Whisking smoothies, what a sight!
Slicing fruits with all their might,
Flavor explosions, pure delight!

A yellow slip; oh what a fall!
Giggles echo through it all.
Slip and slide, what a mess,
Even monkeys feel the stress!

Under bright and glowing sun,
Everyone's invited—come on, run!
Join the feast, don't be shy,
Wipe those tears, and laugh, oh my!

Golden Moments

Yellow treasures swinging low,
A playful breeze begins to blow.
Mischief lingers here and there,
Laughter tickles, fills the air.

With a grin, a fruit so fine,
Peels away, a twisty line.
Each bite brings a giggle fit,
A fruity dance, we can't resist!

Sliding down the garden path,
Silly antics cause a laugh.
Stumbling friends, a hearty cheer,
"Here comes another!" rings so clear.

Golden moments bright and sweet,
Every smile, a fruity treat.
Joyful shouts, a carnival,
In this place, we can't stand still!

Curved Grandeur

Graceful curves in sunlit lands,
Nature's humor, oh, how it stands!
Bouncing fruits from tree to tree,
Tickling toes, so wild and free.

Chasing shadows, laughter wakes,
Underneath, the ground just quakes.
Rolling fruits, a grand parade,
Who needs circus? We've got shade!

Juggling acts from tiny hands,
Fruity snacks in glorious bands.
Catch a peel, and off you go—
Slipping, sliding, putting on a show!

Curved grandeur of nature's show,
With a twist, we steal the flow.
Mirth and grapes, a dance so bright,
Underneath the shimmering light.

Orchard of Laughter

In an orchard, joy runs wild,
Children dance, each one a child.
Grab a snack, its shape so round,
Silly faces all around!

Tickling leaves and buzzing bees,
Fruits adorn the hearty trees.
Giggles echo, tales unfold,
Adventures shared, the best of gold.

A peal of laughter floats so high,
A crown of fruit, oh my, oh my!
Spinning tales of things gone wrong,
Every slip, a jolly song!

Orchard bright with every hue,
In this place, dreams surely brew.
Banquets held beneath the sun,
Join our feast—there's fun for everyone!

The Flavorful Journey

In a land where yellow smiles peek,
Monkeys dance and frolic, hide and seek.
With every swing, they laugh and cheer,
Tasting sweetness that's oh-so-dear.

A fruit parade rolls down the street,
Squeezed between joy and a sticky treat.
With slippery peels and pranks galore,
Who knew fruit could cause such uproar?

The juice spills tales of laughter and glee,
Sipping sweetness as far as the eye can see.
Each bite's a giggle, oh what a scene,
A flavor adventure, if you know what I mean.

In this land where silliness reigns,
Every munch brings loud refrains.
So come, take a seat, enjoy the fun,
With fruits that sparkle under the sun.

Radiance in the Trees

Up in the branches, snug as a bug,
Swinging around, it's all quite a hug.
The golden globes, they call from above,
Bringing a chuckle, a fruit-filled love.

Silly birds chirp their fruity tunes,
While squirrels juggle with sweet little boons.
Under the leaves where the laughter flows,
Everyone knows how the funny fruit grows.

With every munch, the giggles expand,
A sticky disaster, oh, isn't it grand?
The sun shines down, casts shadows that sway,
A bright, fruity party, come join the play!

So cheer for the tree where the fun does bloom,
And relish in laughter that fills up the room.
A fruity delight that no one can beat,
Radiance found in each comical treat.

Treasures of the Jungle

In the jungle depths, a treasure lies,
Wrapped in laughter, under the skies.
With silly faces and fruity cheer,
The wildest party year after year.

A treasure map marked with giggles galore,
Leading to fruits, oh what's in store!
From slippery slides to trampoline swings,
Who knew the jungle could offer such things?

Critters laugh as they scurry and hop,
Around every corner, they cannot stop.
Joyful chaos with every bright bite,
A treasure hunt bathed in golden light.

In this jungle where laughter is key,
Every fruit whispers, "Come play with me!"
So join the fun, don't let it slip,
For treasure like this is worth the trip.

The Melodic Grove

In a grove alive with vibrant noise,
Fruits play instruments, a band of joys.
With pluck and strum, they rock the day,
Making the silliest sounds in play.

Bouncy pears and giggling grapes,
Dancing around without any scrapes.
A swinging beat in the fresh, warm air,
Who knew fruit could be such a flair?

Each note a burst of sunshine and fun,
The laughter echoes till the day is done.
Join in the rhythm of fruity delight,
A melodic grove that feels just right.

So sway to the music, let it unfold,
In this grove of giggles, young and old.
With every bite, join the fruity choir,
A concert of joy that will never tire.

Golden Notes of Nature

In jungles where the laughter grows,
Monkeys dance in charming prose.
With yellow hats upon their heads,
They share their fruity, silly spreads.

Bouncing on vines like jolly clowns,
They roll and jiggle in leafy gowns.
Nutty jokes in every peel,
A fruity feast, what a big meal!

Swinging high in trees so tall,
Their raucous giggles, a joyful call.
Sunshine beams on their golden find,
Nature's treasure, sweetly entwined.

So when you hear their playful cheer,
Know fruity fun is always near.
In every twist, a surprise awaits,
In this land of tasty plate states.

A Symphony of Yellow

In the orchard where the giggles bloom,
Mischiefs swirl in a fruity room.
With trumpets made of peels so bright,
They play the tunes of pure delight.

Coconut hats make perfect crowns,
As they twirl around in silly gowns.
Their melodies bounce from tree to tree,
Join in the dance, come sing with me!

From morning mist to evening's glow,
Their cheerful songs put on a show.
With swinging vines as their grand stage,
They perform antics that never age.

In this concert under the sun,
Every note and laugh is pure fun.
With fruity beats that tickle the air,
Join the symphony, if you dare!

The Luscious Canopy

Under the leaves where shadows play,
Creatures scamper and prance all day.
Yellow snacks from branches high,
That make the whole jungle laugh and sigh.

With cheeky smiles and playful grins,
They toss their treats, let the fun begin!
The canopy shivers with giggly glee,
As friends indulge in a fruity spree.

Each bite brings cheers, a zing, a zing!
Joyful creatures hopping, doing their thing.
Under this roof of green delight,
They revel till the fall of night.

So let's join in this grand parade,
Where every smile is a joyful trade.
In this lush playground, come take a chance,
And join the whimsy of the fruit dance!

Winds of the Tropics

Winds whisper secrets through leaves so bold,
Tales of tangy treasures unfold.
With a swish and sway, and gusts of cheer,
Fruity fun lingers ever near.

Laughter flits on a bat's swift wing,
As sunny tones in the breeze gently sing.
The playful rustle, a humorous tease,
Tropical tunes that dance in the breeze.

From shadowy canopies, shadows peek,
As nature's smiles play hide and seek.
Their games are ripe with silly schemes,
Filling the air with fruity dreams.

So let us twirl with the winds so free,
Join the merry, wild jubilee.
In every breeze, a giggle flows,
In waves of laughter, joy always grows!

Sun-Kissed Yellow Treasures

In the jungle, a treasure found,
Bright and yellow, they dance around.
Curvy smiles on every face,
Mischief lurks in this fruity place.

Peels slip off in a playful way,
Fruity laughter fills the day.
Chasing monkeys in the trees,
Sticky fingers, oh what a tease!

Jungle parties, so much fun,
A fruit fiesta, second to none.
Limbo contests with a twist,
Who could resist this yellow bliss?

Now for cake, we make a spread,
With every slice, joy is led.
Happiness in every bite,
Sun-kissed treasures, pure delight!

The Harvest of Happiness

In the orchard, merriment grows,
With giggles in every row.
Silly hats upon our heads,
As we gather down the spreads.

Baskets full of yellow cheer,
Making smoothies, oh dear, oh dear!
Splatters happen, a fruity fight,
Yummy chaos, pure delight!

Giggles echo, tales unfold,
Of adventures brave and bold.
The harvest dance we all will do,
With fruit confetti flung at you!

Now we feast, the laughter swells,
In a world where joy excels.
We'll toast to what we've come to make,
In this bright, yellow, joy-filled cake!

Lush Layers of Sunshine

A bright delight upon the plate,
Layers stacked, oh isn't fate great?
Whipped up dreams, so creamy and sweet,
Every slice a joyous treat!

Rolling hills of fruity fun,
Underneath the glowing sun.
Races to the juicing machine,
Sticky hands and faces gleam!

Songs of laughter fill the air,
As we mix without a care.
Twirling, spinning, we all cheer,
For our sunshine slice, so dear!

When the party comes to close,
With plenty left, we all suppose.
More for tomorrow, oh what a score,
This sunny layer we can't ignore!

Whispers of the Golden Grove

Deep in the grove, secrets hum,
Golden whispers, here they come!
Fruity friends with tales to share,
Swinging wildly in the air.

A playful breeze shakes the leaves,
In this sticky fun, who believes?
Catch a peel, the laughter flies,
In every nook, a surprise lies!

Sunbeams dance upon the ground,
In this fruity world, joy is found.
Bring your friends and play along,
In the golden grove, we belong!

When day turns dusk, the fun won't cease,
With every nibble, laughter's peace.
Come back tomorrow, we'll do it all,
This fruity paradise, we will enthrall!

The Swaying Symphony

In a grove where fruits collide,
Yellow giggles bounce with pride,
Leaves dance to a quirky beat,
Nature's laughter, oh so sweet.

Jungle jokes in every sway,
Chirpy birds join the fray,
Monkeys swing and tease their mates,
Creating joy that captivates.

With each twist and silly turn,
Lessons of fun we discern,
Playful rhythms fill the air,
Turning frowns to smiles laid bare.

So join the festive, cheerful scene,
Nature's charm, a vibrant green,
In this grove of merry cheer,
Dance along, the fun is here!

Nature's Rich Banquet

Underneath the golden sun,
Fruits parade, a feast for fun,
Laughter mingles with the breeze,
A smorgasbord of joy and ease.

Dancing squirrels steal a bite,
While the parrots take to flight,
Every petal, every leaf,
Holds a story of belief.

Oops! A slip on juicy ground,
Wobbling like a party clown,
Giggling echoes through the trees,
Nature's banquet aims to please.

So take your plate and join the cheer,
Delightful treats are waiting here,
In this feast where fun is sown,
Leave your worries far from home!

Whispering Tropics

In the tropics where winds play,
Whispers of joy come out to stay,
Sunshine tickles every tree,
A funny dance, come, watch with me!

Fronds fluttering soft and light,
Create shadows dancing bright,
Every footfall brings a grin,
As nature twirls us right on in.

Join the laughter of the breeze,
Swaying about with perfect ease,
Melodies in every laugh,
Tropical fun, our hearts' true path.

So waddle with your goofy style,
Let the moments stretch a while,
In this paradise so spry,
Whisper sweetly, don't be shy!

Woven in Gold

Fields of gold, the colors shine,
A playful twist, oh what a line,
Laughter cracked in every clump,
With each harvest comes a thump.

Tiny hands with sticky glee,
Collecting joy as they run free,
Giggles burst like summer rain,
In this treasure, joy we gain.

Sticky fingers, racing fun,
Grapes will roll and hearts will run,
Embrace the mirth in every fold,
Collect the laughter, woven gold.

So grab a handful, share the cheer,
Life's best moments all gathered here,
In this golden, merry fold,
Laughter thrives; our stories told.

A Serenade of Sweetness

In a world full of cheer, you will find,
A fruit that dances, oh so kind.
With a yellow coat and a playful grin,
It peels away woes, let the fun begin.

Oh, slip on a peel, watch your step,
Humor lies where we all prep.
A snack for the brave, a treat for the bold,
In laughter, this fruit's story is told.

Bunches hanging, ripe and bright,
A jester's delight, what a sight!
Chasing away all the gloom,
Creating joy in every room.

So let us toast with a fruity cheer,
To the one who brings us all near.
In laughter and sweetness, take a bite,
For this fruit surely brings delight!

Taste of the Tropics

In the heart of the sun, things are great,
A fruity treasure on every plate.
With smiles so wide, we will munch,
This tropical feast is fit for a bunch.

Swinging from trees in the breeze,
Joking with nature, aiming to please.
Each yellow curve holds a wink,
A splash of joy on the cusp of a drink.

In smoothies we blend, with style and flair,
Catching giggles in the warm, salty air.
Let's peel it back and have a laugh,
As we savor nature's fruity craft.

So gather around with a playful heart,
From the garden of laughter, let's take part.
With each juicy bite, let's raise a cheer,
To the playful gift that draws us here!

Ripened Dreams Under the Sun

Under bright skies where the laughter flows,
A golden delight with a playful nose.
Dreams of sweetness drift and sway,
In the orchard of giggles, come what may.

The flappers dance in the evening light,
As munchkins giggle, what a sight!
With a wink and a peel, we take a dare,
To indulge in the joy hanging in the air.

Each squishy bite bursts with cheer,
As shadows lengthen, spreading delight near.
No frowns allowed in this fruity spree,
For giggles are gathered, wild and free.

In sunlit realms, let's swish and sway,
Chasing our troubles cheer away.
With fruity roads ahead, full of fun,
Let's celebrate till the day is done!

The Lure of the Sunlit Orchard

In the orchard where laughter grows,
A sunny treat that everyone knows.
With smiles so wide and spirits high,
We savor the joy as we swing and fly.

Curves and colors in a cheerful dance,
Each fruit invites us to take a chance.
With giggles that sparkle in the air,
We dive into fun without a care.

When the sun sets low and dreams ignite,
A harvest of laughter is our delight.
So gather your friends for a fun-filled stint,
In the rich golden glow, let's munch and sprint.

With bows and banter, let's make a toast,
To the joy that we cherish and love the most.
In this playful journey, we find our thrill,
Together in sweetness, we'll always spill!

Cozy Canopy Conversations

In the leaves, we gather round,
Whispers sweet, a silly sound.
Chattering critters, dressed so bright,
Swinging wishes in the light.

Laughter echoes, a playful tease,
As the breeze dances through the trees.
A fruit with chuckles, joy so rare,
Sipping sunshine, without a care.

Chatter of monkeys, flip and swing,
Swinging jokes, what joy they bring!
With every giggle, a peel in sight,
Cozy canopy, pure delight!

Join the fun, come take your place,
Under the leaves, a merry space.
Let's mold the laughter, bright and green,
In this fruity, friendly scene.

The Serpent of Sweetness

Slyly lurking in the shade,
A creature with a charm displayed.
Twisting tales, oh what a sight,
With a wiggly grin, it dances light.

It's not a snake, but glows like gold,
A sweetness lurking, brave and bold.
With every twist, it grabs a smile,
Oh such antics, mile by mile.

Gather 'round and share the cheer,
As the little serpent draws us near.
In this jungle where joy will speak,
The funny tales play hide and seek.

Laughing together, a fruity tease,
As the serpent sways in the breeze.
Let sweetness shine, in every jest,
With every giggle, we feel so blessed.

Tropical Treasury

Beneath the palm, treasures lie,
Shiny and yellow, oh me, oh my!
Gathering giggles, laughter galore,
In this tropical place, who could ask for more?

Coconuts chuckle, shells all around,
In our bright kingdom, where joy is found.
Every morsel comes with a wink,
In this quirky spot, we'll never sink.

Dive in the bounty, feel the fun,
With every bite, we dance and run.
Golden delights, on this sunny quest,
In a place where we laugh, we are truly blessed.

Come share the treasure, full of cheer,
A tropical world, where all draw near.
With every giggle, the bounty grows,
In this silly land, where laughter flows.